# Pancakes

Mary O'Keeffe

How do we get **pancakes**? What is in a **pancake**? Let's go and mix some up!

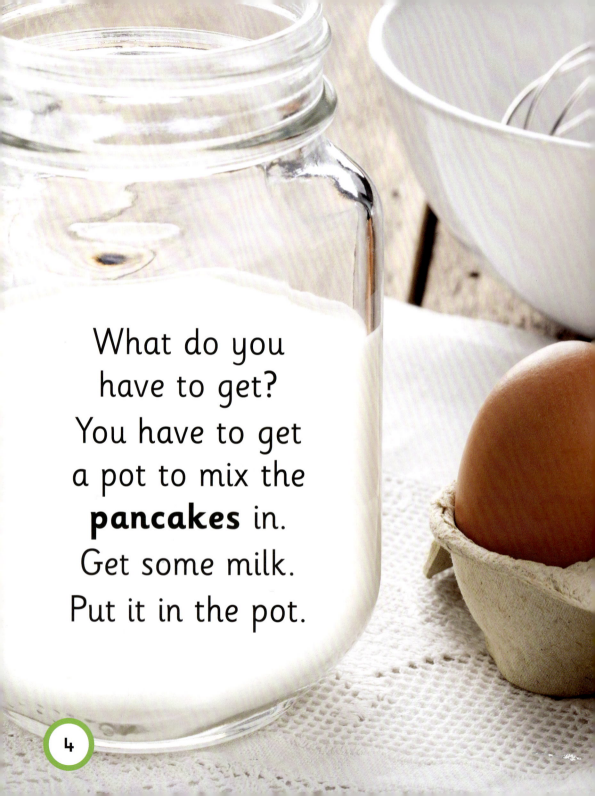

What do you have to get? You have to get a pot to mix the **pancakes** in. Get some milk. Put it in the pot.

It is fun!

Get a cup.
You will have to sift it in.

You will have to mix it up so there are no lumps.

You have **pancake** batter.

You have to get a pan. You have to let it get hot.

Put on some butter. Let it melt.

It is hot, so you have
to get some help.
Put some batter on the pan.
Do you like big **pancakes**
or little ones?

When you see them pop up, you can toss your **pancake**. Put the pan down and then put it up quick!

Did it land back in the pan?
Let's get some more
**pancakes** on the pan!

The pan has to be a little hot.

His **pancake** did not burn.

It will be yum!

Oh no! Her **pancake** did burn!

She did not turn down her pan.

The **pancake** has to go in the bin!

She will have to put on some more!

Make sure you fry your pancake on medium heat!

Can you sing my song?

'Mix a **pancake**,
Mix a **pancake**,
Pop it in a pan!'

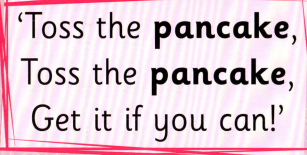

'Toss the **pancake**,
Toss the **pancake**,
Get it if you can!'

Yes!

Now we can mix up some **pancake** batter.
We can toss **pancakes**.
Let's go and have some more!
What can we put on top?